THE
SEPTEMBER
BABY

By Noel Streatfeild and available from Headline

The January Baby

The February Baby

The March Baby

The April Baby

The May Baby

The June Baby

The July Baby

The August Baby

The September Baby

The October Baby

The November Baby

The December Baby

THE
September
BABY

★

Noel Streatfeild

First published in 1959
This edition published in 2023 by Headline Home
an imprint of Headline Publishing Group

1

Cataloguing in Publication Data is available from the British Library

Hardback ISBN 978 1 0354 0855 9
eISBN 978 1 0354 0856 6

Typeset in 14.75/15pt Centaur MT Pro by Jouve (UK), Milton Keynes

Printed and bound in Great Britain by Clays Ltd, Elcograf S.p.A.

HEADLINE PUBLISHING GROUP
An Hachette UK Company
Carmelite House
50 Victoria Embankment
London EC4Y 0DZ

www.headline.co.uk
www.hachette.co.uk

CONTENTS

SEPTEMBER is the golden month: golden fields of corn, vivid yellow flowers in the hedgerows, and by the end of the month the first leaves on the trees are turning gold. A lovely month in which to be born. What a ringing of telephones and a writing of letters your September baby has caused, and now the moment has arrived when you are to be allowed visitors, and the question is being asked, 'What present shall I bring her?'

It is likely the September baby and its mother will be given presents bought during holidays. As relatives and friends gather round, their complexions varying from beetroot to that strange chrome shade that disastrously follows tan, parcels from far away places should cover the bed. It is to be hoped they are all delightful, but this is unlikely, for

as we all know what seemed to be a perfect present in that dear little shop in Austria, or bought from that fascinating man in Istanbul, seldom looks so well chosen when unpacked back home. That scent especially blended, which smelt divine at the time of purchase, reaches England with a manure under-smell, and that cute baby's bonnet which you spent so much on, you can feel in your bones the September baby will never be allowed to wear.

And, oh dear, those carved animals were
definitely a mistake, and so was that weird
bottle of Greek liquor.

Gifts from away apart, September is an
awkward month for presents. Apart from
the fact that holidays have left everybody
flat broke, the ordinary presents are
difficult. September is not a good month
for flowers, except for chrysanthemums and
michaelmas daisies, and it is aggravating to
have spent more than can easily be spared
on a dozen perfect chrysanthemums, only

to find the room or ward already bursting with other dozens of the same shade and perfection.

Bedjackets make nice presents, and September is a good month to give them, for so often a little something extra to slip on is wanted when the evenings are drawing in,

and it is not yet late enough in the year for fires. And of course nothing can be more perfect as a present than an outfit for baby, but which of us is strong-minded enough to keep such gifts until the baby has arrived?

The temptation is so great to post them on the day we finished making them.

It is years of facing this problem, 'What shall I give her?' that has resulted in this book. Obviously there is only one subject of conversation, and that is the new baby. So here, collected in a small book is information about September babies.

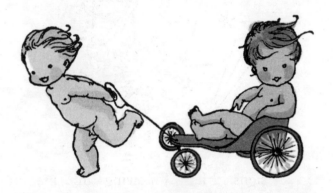

The book opens with names vaguely connected with September. It seems odd, but experience has shown that many parents are thankful for names. Often the first name for one reason or another is a foregone conclusion, but then the difficulty arises that it goes abominably with the surname, and in any case another name or two are wanted. Thus the list.

Although we may scorn information about what the stars foretell, few of us can resist the

zodiac signs. Here following information about your baby – whether it was born under the sign of Virgo or Libra – there follows a list of some of the distinguished born on each day in September, and should you have time to read it, very surprising reading you will find it. Take the eighteenth: how very odd that Greta Garbo, that retiring exquisite actress, could share a birthday with Samuel

Johnson, one of the greatest talkers that ever lived. Or the twenty-third — admittedly one belonged to fifth century Athens B.C., and the other belongs to twentieth century America A.D., but who could guess that Euripides and Mickey Rooney would share a birthday? Which, I wonder, of those who share a birthday with your September baby, would you most dislike, or like, it to resemble?

NAMES
for the
SEPTEMBER
BABY

THE sign of the zodiac for part of September is Libra, the Scales, which are the symbol of justice; *Justin* and *Justina* both mean 'just'. A judgment is supposed to be just, so here are some names connected with judgment. *Reginald*, *Reynold* and *Ronald* for boys, and *Rona* for a girl mean 'powerful judgment'. *Renfred* means 'judgement of peace'. *Daniel* means 'God is my judge'. *Dinah* means 'judged'. Linked with justice are *Mercy* and *Charity*, both charming names for girls. Scales or a balance suggest deciding as well as justice. *Angus* means 'one choice', and *Fergus* 'manly choice'. Counsel are usually connected with the giving of judgment; *Aubrey* and *Alfred* mean 'crafty counsellor', *Conrad* 'bold counsel', *Rayner* 'counsel folk', and *Redmond* 'counsel-protection.' Two names which ought to be associated with counsel are *Cato* 'sagacious' and *Hubert* which means 'of bright mind'. (*Hew, Hugh, Hugo* and *Huw* mean 'mind'.) For girls *Sophia, Sophie* and *Sophy* mean 'wisdom', *Sonia* means 'wise', and *Melinda* 'sweetly wise'. Justice and Truth go together, so how about *Verity, Alethea, Alice, Alicen, Alicia, Alison* and *Alys*, all of which mean 'truth'? *Verena* and *Veronica* mean 'true image'. *Nora, Norah* and *Noreen*, meaning 'honour' in the sense of 'reputation', are the shortened forms of *Honor, Honora* and *Honoria.*

September is the beginning of the hunting season, so how about the boy's name *Hunt? Errol* and *Wendy* both mean 'wanderer', and two other names of an old-world type which suggest hunting are *Rebecca* which means 'noosed cord' and *Evadne* 'well-tamed'. In the early days of history while the men were out hunting, the women had to stay at home, so here are some names connected

with home. *Penelope* means 'weaver', *Sidony* 'fine cloth', and *Etta, Harriet* and *Henrietta* 'home-ruler'. The Greek name *Hero* fits in here, it means 'mistress of the house', and *Vesta* means 'hearth'. Thinking of hearth, here are three names which mean 'fire': *Aine,*

Aithne and *Ena*. For those who wish to get away from hearths, *Fanny*, *Frances* and *Francesca* mean 'free', and *Barbara* means 'a stranger'. But returning to the hearth-side again, *Prudence* is a suitable name for the home, or *Ivy* which clings to the walls. Here is a list of the more homely qualities, which may give some ideas for naming a September baby. *Agatha* means 'good', *Monica* 'unique', *Alma* 'kind', *Althea* 'wholesome', *Dilys* 'genuine', *Dulcie* 'sweet', *Elvina* 'friendly', *Haidee* 'modest', and *Moira* 'soft'. *Netta* and *Nita* mean 'sweet', *Serena* 'calm', and *Eve* or *Eva* 'lively'.

Every month has a special apostle assigned to it. The one for September is Lebbeus Thaddeus. *Thaddeus*, though it's an unlikely name for your baby son, means 'praise', and another form of it is *Jude* which means 'praised'.

The 1st of September is St Giles' Day. *Giles* means 'kid'.

The 17th of September is St Lambert's Day. *Lambert* itself means 'land-bright', but there are many names which end in 'bert', so take a look at some of them. *Albert* 'nobly bright',

Bertram and *Bertrand* 'bright raven', *Colbert* 'cool brightness', *Cuthbert* 'famous brightness', *Egbert*, a Saxon name, 'sword-bright', *Filbert* (which does not mean a nut), 'exceeding bright', *Gerbert* 'bright spear', *Gilbert* 'bright pledge', *Herbert* 'bright army', *Humbert* 'bright giant', *Norbert* 'Niord's brightness', *Osbert* 'divinely bright', and *Robert* 'bright fame'.

St Matthew's Day is the 21st of September, when the days and nights are of equal length, and the tides are so low that they uncover treasures usually hidden under the sea. *Matthew* means 'gift of Jehovah'. Three other names also meaning 'God's gift' are *Nathaniel*, *Theodore*, and *Theodora* for a girl.

The 28th of September is St Cyprian's Day. *Cyprian* means 'of Cyprus'.

The 29th of September is the day of St Michael and All Angels. *Michael* means 'Who is like to God'. *Carmichael* means 'friend of Michael'. *Angel* means 'messenger', in the heavenly sense, and has been used as a boy's name, and though there are no female angels in the Bible, there are feminine forms of the name – *Angela*, *Angelica* and *Angelina*. If you think of angels, you think of Gabriel and

Raphael. *Gabriel* means 'strong man of God', and *Raphael* 'medicine of God'.

Michaelmas Day is the day for settling accounts, so how about *Penny* for a baby girl? Thinking about money, *Odo* and *Otto* mean 'rich', and *Edwin* and *Edwina* mean 'rich friend',

Edna 'rich gift', *Edward* 'rich ward', *Eamon*, *Edmond* and *Edmund* all mean 'rich protection'.

September's flower is the morning glory, so *Glory* or *Gloria* are September names, but if you would like to be original how about *Dahlia*? For dahlias are at their best in September, and it would make a charming name.

GIFTS
for the
SEPTEMBER
BABY

IF a godparent or other well-wisher would like to give the baby a piece of jewellery, the right stone for September is the sapphire. Mothers of September babies will probably sigh, and wish that their offspring had not chosen such an opulent stone, and will discourage their baby from drinking its sapphires in milk, as Leonardus suggests. Here is what he wrote in 1750 about its properties in *The Mirror of Stones*:

'It refreshes the Body, and gives a good Colour; it checks the Ardor of Lust, and makes a Person chaste and virtuous, and restrains too much Sweat. It takes away the Filth of the Eyes and the Pains of the Head. Being drank with Milk, it appeases the Gripes of the Belly. It renders the Bearer of it pacifick, amiable, pious and devout, and confirms the Soul in good Works. It discovers Frauds; expels Terrors. It is of great Service in magic Arts, and is said to be of prodigious Efficacy in the Works of Necromancy. It discharges a Carbuncle with a single Touch. The Eyes being touch'd with it, it preserves them from being injur'd by the Small-Pox.'

The charming old custom of arranging flowers in a vase or bunch so that it brings a message is neglected nowadays. But if your baby should receive a bunch of agrimony and mallow, the message it brings is Thankfulness (agrimony) and Beneficence (mallow).

If your baby was born between the 1st and the 23rd of September read pages 24 and 25, but if between the 24th and the 30th skip to pages 26 and 27.

UNDER
WHAT STARS WAS
MY BABY
BORN?

VIRGO
The Virgin
24th August–23rd September

LIBRA
The Scales
24th September–23rd October

SCORPIO
The Scorpion
24th October–22nd November

SAGITTARIUS
The Archer
23rd November–21st December

CAPRICORN
The Sea Goat
22nd December–20th January

AQUARIUS
The Water Bearer
21st January–19th February

PISCES
The Fishes
20th February–20th March

ARIES
The Ram
21st March–20th April

TAURUS
The Bull
21st April–21st May

GEMINI
The Twins
22nd May–21st June

CANCER
The Crab
22nd June–23rd July

LEO
The Lion
24th July–23rd August

Virgo — the Virgin
24th August–23rd September

THE chief characteristic of Virgo persons is inward purity. They are going very much against the grain when they do not match this purity of mind with chastity. Whatever their lives externally, they do not cease to be of spiritual imagination. Equally endowed with intuition and with practical reasoning power and ingenuity, they are among the cleverest of the twelve types. They are studious, and conscientious to a worrisome degree. Virgo people are quite likely to have wit, but unlikely to have a sense of humour. A certain quality of detachment makes them slow to form friendships and not sure to maintain them. They have a tremendous capacity for devotion, but such a tendency to idealise and demand perfection of the people they love as to make for a stormy emotional life.

For the Virgo Baby

Lucky to wear topaz, amber.
Lucky stones are marble, glass.
Lucky metal is quicksilver.
The Virgo baby's colour is yellow.
Lucky number is 5.
Luckiest day is Wednesday.

Libra — the Scales
24th September–23rd October

THE special characteristic of people born under Libra is intuition. They have great breadth of perception and not so much a lack of the power to reason as a lack of the necessity to do so, so thoroughly can they depend upon intuitive acuteness. Librans are refined and unassuming, demonstratively affectionate, and easily influenced by others. When in uncongenial surroundings they are more apt to look for solace within themselves than to muster the energy needed to change their circumstances. They lack physical strength too, though their bodies are likely to be of unusually harmonious proportions. Librans are disquieted by injustice and may find a career in combatting it. They have a ready weapon in their outstanding grace of elocution.

For the Libra Baby

Lucky to wear an opal.
Lucky stones are malachite, turquoise.
Lucky metal is copper.
The Libra baby's colour is green.
Lucky number is 6.
Luckiest day is Friday.

BABIES BORN
ON
THE SAME DAY
AS
YOUR BABY

IS there a special advantage in being born on a particular day? Is there any truth in horoscopes and what the stars foretell? Will babies born under the sign of Virgo grow up to be like this, and those born under the sign of Libra like that? Here is a list of well-known people from every part of history and from every sphere of life, which will help you to decide.

1st   Marguerite Gardiner, Countess of Blessington, 1789. Air Chief Marshal Sir Frederick Bowhill, 1880.
2nd   Caroline Schlegel-Shelling, 1763. Frederick Soddy, 1877. Sir Robert Bruce Lockhart, 1887.

3rd   Matthew Boulton, 1728. Prince Eugène de Beauharnais, 1781. Jean Léon Jaurès, 1859. Sir Macfarlane Burnet, 1899.

4th   Pindar, 518 B.C. Alexander III of Scotland, 1241. Chateaubriand, 1768. Anton Bruckner, 1824. Darius Milhaud, 1892. Sylvia Thompson, 1902.

5th   Louis XIV of France, 1638. Giacomo Meyerbeer, 1791. Sir S. Radhakrishnan, 1888. Margaret Popham, 1894. Arthur Koestler, 1905.

6th   Marquis de Lafayette, 1757. John Dalton, 1766. Georges Picquart, 1854. Sir Barry Jackson, 1879.

7th   Elizabeth I, 1533. Count de Buffon, 1707. Sir Henry Campbell-Bannerman, 1836. Lieut.-Gen. Sir Brian Horrocks, 1895. Anthony Quayle, 1913. Group Capt. Cheshire, 1917. Baudouin I, King of the Belgians, 1930.

8th   Richard I 'The Lion-Hearted,' 1157. Lodovico Ariosto, 1474. Princess de Lamballe, 1749. Dvořák, 1841. Siegfried Sassoon, 1886. Huseyn Shaheed

Suhrawardy, 1892. Dorothy Dix, 1910. Jean-Louis Barrault, 1910.

9th   Cardinal Richelieu, 1585. Galvani, 1737. Captain Bligh, 1754. Tolstoy, 1828. Peter Traill, 1896. Emile Littler, 1903.

10th   Maria Theresa of Austria, 1638. Mungo Park, 1771. Franz Werfel, 1890.

11th   Margaret, Duchess of Brabant, 1275. Turenne, 1611. Joanna Baillie, 1762. Vinobha Bhave, 1895. Lord Byng of Vimy, 1862. O. Henry, 1862. Sir James Jeans, 1877. D. H. Lawrence, 1885. Field-Marshal Sir Gerald Templer, 1898. Herbert Lom, 1917.

12th   Francis I of France, 1494. Lord Oxford and Asquith, 1852. Maurice Chevalier, 1888. Irène Joliot-Curie, 1897. Louis MacNeice, 1907. Han Suyin, 1916.

13th   William Cecil, Lord Burghley, 1520. Arthur Henderson, 1863. Lord Birdwood, 1865. J. B. Priestley, 1894. Claudette Colbert, 1903.

14th   Baron Alexander von Humboldt, 1769. Jan Masaryk, 1886. Peter Scott, 1909. Jack Hawkins, 1910.

15th   James Fenimore Cooper, 1789. Ernest Crofts, 1847. Jean Renoir, 1894. Margaret Lockwood, 1916.

16th   Henry V, 1387. Tintoretto, 1518. Baron Rothschild, 1777. Bonar Law, 1858. Alfred Noyes, 1880. Sir Alexander Korda, 1893. Lauren Bacall, 1924.

17th   Condorcet, 1743. Hartley Coleridge, 1796. Frederick Ashton, 1906. Ursula Howells, 1922. Stirling Moss, 1929.

18th   Samuel Johnson, 1709. Sir Owen Seaman, 1861. Fay Compton, 1894. John G. Diefenbaker, 1895. Greta Garbo, 1905.

19th   Arthur, Prince of Wales, 1486. Lajos Kossuth, 1802. William Dyce, 1806. George Cadbury, 1839.

20th   Henry Fitzroy, 1st Duke of Grafton, 1663. General Gamelin, 1872. Sister Kenny, 1886. Sir Robert Heatlie Scott, 1905. Kenneth More, 1914. Sophia Loren, 1934.

21st   Savonarola, 1452. Dick Turpin, 1705. Louis Bonaparte, King of Holland, 1778. H. G. Wells, 1866. Don Juan de la Cierva, 1895. Capt. Charles H. Upham, V.C. and bar, 1908.

22nd Ann of Cleves, 1515. Anne of Austria, 1601. Lord Chesterfield, 1694. Michael Faraday, 1791. Erich von Stroheim, 1885.

23rd Euripides, 480 B.C. Emperor Octavius Caesar Augustus, 63 B.C. Geoffrey Plantagenet, Count of Bretagne, 1158. Dr Jeremy Collier, 1650. Lord Boyd-Orr, 1880. Walter Pidgeon, 1898. Mickey Rooney, 1920.

24th Sir Howard Florey, 1898. Bessie Braddock, 1899. Sir A. P. Herbert, 1890.

25th Mrs Hemans, 1793. C. B. Cochran, 1872. G. D. H. Cole, 1889. William Faulkner, 1897. Dimitri Shostakovich, 1906.

26th Lord Collingwood, 1750. Martin Heidegger, 1889. George Gershwin, 1898.

27th Louis XIII of France, 1601. Jacques Bossuet, 1627. George Cruikshank, 1792. Admiral of the Fleet, Lord Chatfield, 1873. Basil Dean, 1888. Bernard Miles, 1907.

28th Prosper Mérimée, 1803. Friedrich Engels, 1820. Francis Turner Palgrave,

1824. Georges Clemenceau, 1841. Lord French of Ypres, 1852. Edith Pargeter, 1913. Peter Finch, 1916. Caryl Doncaster, 1923.

29th Margaret, Queen of Scotland, 1240. Clive of India, 1725. Lord Nelson, 1758. Mrs Gaskell, 1812. Trevor Howard, 1916.

30th Jacques Necker, 1732. Lord Roberts, 1832. Hans Geiger, 1882. Michael Powell, 1905. Deborah Kerr, 1921.

THE
UPBRINGING
OF SEPTEMBER
BABIES
OF
THE
PAST

I ELEONER PEAD, admitted to the
Office and Occupation of a Midwife,
will faithfully and diligently exercise
the said Office according to such Cunning
and Knowledge as God hath given me: And
that I will be ready to help and aid as well
Poor as Rich Women being in Labour and
Travail of Child, and will always be ready
both to Poor and Rich, in Exercising and
Executing of my said Office: Also, I will not
permit or suffer that any Woman being in
Labour or Travail shall name any other to be
the Father of her Child, than only he who
is the right and true Father thereof. And
that I will not suffer any other Bodies
Child to be set, brought, or laid before
any Woman delivered of Child in the Place
of her natural Child, so far forth as I can
know and understand. Also, I will not
use any kind of Sorcery or Incantation in
the time of the Travail of any Woman:
And that I will not destroy the Child born
of any Woman, nor cut, nor pull off the

Head thereof, or otherwise dismember or hurt the same, or suffer it to be so hurt, or dismembered by any manner of Ways or Means. Also, that in the Ministration of the Sacrament of Baptism in the time of Necessity, I will use apt and the accustomed Words of the same Sacrament, that is to say, these Words following, or the like in effect, *I Christen thee in the Name of the Father, the Son, and the Holy Ghost,* and none other profane Words. And that in such time of Necessity, in Baptizing any Infant born, and pouring Water upon the Head of the same Infant, I will use pure and clean Water, and not any Rose or Damask Water, or Water made of any Confection or Mixture: And that I will Certify the Curate of the Parish Church of every such Baptizing.

Strype, *Annals,* 1725.

FLANNEL SACQUES

As we have said, sacques of colored flannel have in a great measure superseded the more cumbersome blanket, when the child is large enough to be dressed in them.

They are of the simplest sacque form, loose to the figure and arm, and made of two or three sizes. For the variable temperature of our

climate, in the spring and autumn, they are almost indispensable. Even through the summer, the cool nights and mornings make them a most acceptable fashion. As the child grows large enough to be carried out, they are quite suitable for the street. Sacques are of course made of every material. Merino or cashmere, in plain colors, are preferred by many; but flannel looks best when washed, and the finest white we consider even handsomer than cashmere, when embroidered in silk. It can be had of the most delicate shades, of any color and quality. Buff will perhaps wash best; pale blue, pink, buff and green, are the usual colors chosen; the finest, for special occasions, of white, and done with silk; the others with zephyr worsted, to match the shade, if washing will be frequent. If bound, it is with ribbon; embroidery will be found most serviceable. Suitable flannel can be had at 62c. and 75c. per yard; three quarters of a yard will cut a size suitable for an ordinary child of a year old. They can be fastened at the throat with flat silk buttons, and loops of braid; long, loose sleeves.

The Nursery Basket, New York, 1854.

RICKETS CURE

Steel, as a preventive, has had its warm advocates, who, in order to be able to distinguish whether a child will become rickety, point out the following symptoms: – a paleness and swelling of the countenance, and in that part of the cheeks, which should be naturally red, a yellow colour approaching to that of sulphur; in which case, five grains of the filings of iron, and as much rhubarb, with ten grains of sugar, should be given every morning fasting, and evening – but should this prove too purgative at first, one dose should only be given every day – after a month's continuance, a keen appetite ensues, quick digestion, and a copious flow of urine – the fullness of the face, and yellowness of the complexion, by degrees are removed, and the natural countenance and firmness of the body gradually restored – and this practice, it is said, has never failed of success in any one instance.

Culpeper,
The Complete London Dispensatory, 1802.

CONCERNING THE EXERCISES OF YOUNG CHILDREN

Take Care, that he leave off all Exercise, as soon as his Colour begins to appear in his Face, or any Sweat or Moisture upon his

Skin, for fear lest by continuing it too long, too much of his Spirits, together with the finest Part of his Blood, should be wasted, and so his Growth should be hinder'd. But if the Child be backward in going, because through an Excess of natural Heat, he wastes more of the Nourishment he takes, than he digests, he ought *to drink a Ptisan made of Barley, the Cold Seeds, Apples,* Chiendent, *with Syrup of Water-Lillies, or Limons; which being taken in a small Quantity, will cool him powerfully;* besides which, *he should be purg'd gently with* Cassia, *sweeten'd with a little Sugar, or with a Decoction of* Manna. But if the Child be backward on his Feet, because his Legs, for want of sufficient Nourishment, are not strong enough to support the rest of his Body, they ought to be rubb'd gently with the Hand, 'till they begin to swell, and look reddish; and then a *Cerecloth of Sanders* ought to be apply'd to 'em, to contract the Pores of the Skin, and to cool the Blood that was brought into 'em by rubbing, and by that Means prevent its Evaporation.

The Nurse's Guide, by an Eminent Physician, London, 1729.

43

It is customary to give children bread
and butter for their breakfast, and indeed
whenever their appetite is craving; butter
is exceedingly pernicious for children; a
bason of thick water-gruel, with a small
quantity of milk and treacle, or occasionally
rice and milk, would be infinitely more
nourishing, equally palatable, and con-
siderably cheaper. It would be also a good
supper for children, or for the sake of
variety, bread and milk, which is better for
supper than breakfast, as at night it tends
to help repose, but in the morning will

create sluggishness. Children should never have cheese for dinner or supper, as it is exceedingly unwholesome for their tender stomachs; nor should they ever have raw milk (as is frequently the custom) to drink, as it engenders worms; and if occasionally indulged with fish for dinner, they should have no milk for supper, as fish and milk never agree.

Culpeper,
The Complete London Dispensatory, 1802.

When a child is afflicted with rupture, grease it with lard from a fox, and the rupture will soon heal.

Albertus Magnus, *White and Black Art for Man and Beast*, 13th Century.

SEPARATION OF THE BOYS AND GIRLS. — After the assembling of the school, the first division that takes place must be that of the boys and the girls, whom it will be well to arrange at the opposite sides of the rooms. It may, indeed, seem useless to insist on this division among children so young as those at an infants' school; nor

45

am I prepared to say that there is an absolute
and present necessity for it. The principle,
however, is accordant with the system. In
such an establishment, regard must be paid
to the *appearance* and the *tendency* of things, as
well as to their present nature; and the
arrangement which I have thus recommended
will, amongst others, encourage a delicacy
of mind and propriety of manners, which
the children will probably never totally
forget.

Wilson, *System of Infants' Schools*, 1825.

DUTCH SCHOOL-RELICS. — Some days ago we had in Amsterdam an exhibition of objects either belonging or having belonged to school-management and school discipline. Amongst the objects, dating from a former *régime*, were a *ferula* and *the semblance of a bird.* The mode of application was this: the bird was thrown to the offender, who had to take it back-to the schoolmaster in order to receive his destined share of slaps on the palm of the hand. There besides were *an iron comb,* to unravel stubborn and uncultivated hairs, *a fool's cap with bells and asses's ears, a wooden block for penitence, a painted piece of board, on which an ass's head,* to hang over the chest, &c.

A Correspondent to
Notes and Queries, September 1860.

Factory labour is a species of work, in some respects singularly unfitted for children. Cooped up in a heated atmosphere, debarred the necessary exercise, remaining in one position for a series of hours, one set or system of muscles alone called into activity, it cannot be wondered at — that its effects are injurious to the physical growth of a child.

47

Where the bony system is still imperfect, the vertical position it is compelled to retain, influences its direction; the spinal column bends beneath the weight of the head, bulges out laterally, or is dragged forward by the weight of the parts composing the chest, the pelvis yields beneath the opposing pressure downwards, and the resistance given by the thigh-bones; its capacity is lessened, sometimes more and sometimes less; the legs curve, and the whole body loses height, in consequence of this general yielding and bending of its parts.

Gaskell, *The Manufacturing Population of England*, 1833.

An abstract from the statutes of the Manchester Free Grammar School, the foundation charter of 1525:

Acts and Ordinaunces concnyng the Scollers.
1st. That 'no scoller nor infaunt, of what cuntrey or schire so ev. he be of, beyng man child, be refused,' except he have some infectious disease, 'wiche be, and shal alwaies be remytted to the discresion of the Warden or Deputie of Manchester Collige for the tyme beyng.'

2nd. Must assist the master or usher when commanded.

3rd. Must not wear any dagger, hanger, or other weapon, nor bring into the school any 'staffe or bate,' except the meat knives.

4th. States the punishment of any scholar making 'an affray' upon the master, usher, or any of the other scholars.

5th. Prohibits unlawful games.

6th and 7th. That the master, usher, and scholars should be in school before seven o'clock in the morning between Michaelmas and Easter, and at six o'clock between Easter and Michaelmas, except 'such as come dayly fer to their lernyng,' who should attend at such hour as the master should name.

8th. Every scholar to pay on admission one penny to the two poor children who were to keep the book of names.

9th. No scholar to bring meat or drink into the school, but, if necessary, must eat or drink in some house in the town.

10th. Provides for any scholar leaving the school for another.

11th. The scholars to speak Latin in the school, 'and all other places convenyaunt.'

Now though we have given you large
commendations of this quarter, yet there is
one day in it, of which I would warn you to
have special care, and that is Holy-Rood
day; in which, they say, the Devil goes a
nutting: therefore all you women who love
your children, keep them strictly at home
that day, for fear they meet with the cloven

foot'd friend: nay, rather send your husbands, whom you may best spare, for you may have more husbands, but are not sure you shall have more children.

Poor Robin's Almanack, 1790.

TWO
ROYAL SEPTEMBER
BABIES

HENRY V
born September 1387.

HENRY was extremely fond of
music, and this taste was cultivated
at a very early age; in proof
whereof, the household-book of his grandsire,
John of Gaunt, may be cited. New strings
were purchased for the harp of the young
hero before he was ten years old. About the
same time there is a charge for the scabbard of
his little sword, and for an ounce of black silk
to make his sword-knot; and, moreover, four
shillings were expended in seven books of
grammar for his use, bound up in one volume.

Strickland,
Lives of the Queens of England, 1875.

ELIZABETH I
born September 1533.

Now it is so, my lady Elizabeth is put from that degree she was afore, and what degree she is at now, I know not but by hearsay. Therefore I know not how to order her, nor myself, nor none of hers that I have the rule of, – that is, her women and grooms, beseeching you to be good lord to my lady, and to all hers, and that she may have some raiment.

She hath neither gown, nor kirtle, nor petticoat, nor no manner of linen, – nor forsmocks, nor kerchiefs, nor rails, nor body-stichets, nor handkerchiefs, nor sleeves, nor mufflers, nor biggens. All these her grace must take. I have driven off as long as I can, that by my troth, I can drive it off no longer.

From a letter written by her governess, when Elizabeth was three years old.

DISTINGUISHED
SEPTEMBER
BABIES

born September 1709.

THE christening of his brother he remembered with all its circumstances, and said, his mother taught him to spell and pronounce the words *little Natty*, syllable by syllable, making him say it over in the evening to her husband and his guests. The trick which most parents play with their children, that of shewing off their newly-acquired accomplishments, disgusted Mr Johnson beyond expression; he had been treated so himself, he said, till he absolutely loathed his father's caresses, because he knew they were sure to precede some unpleasing display of his early abilities; and he used, when neighbours came o'visiting, to run up a tree that he might not be found and exhibited, such, as no doubt he was, a prodigy of early understanding. His epitaph upon the duck he killed by treading on it at five years old,

Here lies poor duck
That Samuel Johnson trod on;

If it had liv'd it had been good luck,
    For it would have been an odd one
is a striking example of early expansion of
mind, and knowledge of language; yet he
always seemed more mortified at the recollection of the bustle his parents made with
his wit, than pleased with the thoughts of
possessing it.

Anecdotes of the late Samuel Johnson, LL.D.
by Hesther Lynch Piozzi, 1786.

CLIVE OF INDIA
born September 1725.

He has just had a suit of new clothes, and
promises by his reformation to deserve
them. I am satisfied that his fighting (to
which he is out of measure addicted) gives
his temper a fierceness and imperiousness,
that he flies out upon every trifling occasion:
for this reason I do what I can to suppress
the hero, that I may help forward the more
valuable qualities of meekness, benevolence,
and patience.

From a letter by his uncle, dated 1732.

JOHN DALTON
born September 1766.

Weaver Dalton had in John's infancy
removed three doors higher up the lane, and
upon the outside, or as some say, on the front
door, of this dwelling John posted a large sheet
of white paper, inscribed with a bold hand,
containing the announcement of his having
opened a school for both sexes, and on
reasonable terms. This advertisement long did
duty, and was also accompanied by another to
the effect that 'paper, pens, and ink' were sold
within – two literary acquisitions to Eaglesfield,
springing from the enterprise of a lad of twelve
or thirteen years of age.

For a short while he taught his primitive
school in an old barn, then in his father's
house, and finally in the Friend's Meetinghouse
within the burial-ground enclosure. His
scholars were of all ages, from infancy to
seventeen. Some were so young, that he had
to mount them upon his knee to teach them
their A B C's; others were as old, and much
older and bigger than himself, the proximity
of the school having brought out lots of

Eaglesfield lads whose education and manners had hitherto been grossly neglected. These last-named proved highly refractory scholars; so much so, that when John threatened them with chastisement for neglecting their lessons, or their naughtiness for playing leap-frog over the graves of the dead . . . they rebelled, and actually challenged him out to fight.

Lonsdale, *The Worthies of Cumberland*, 1874.

GEORGE CRUIKSHANK
born September 1792.

Not only did the men in 1803 form themselves into regiments of volunteers, but the boys of that day did so likewise, and my brother (of whom I have already spoken), and who was my elder by three years, formed one of these juvenile regiments, and appointed *himself* the colonel. We had our drum and fife, our 'colours,' presented by our mammas and sisters, who also assisted in making our accoutrements. We also procured small 'gun-stocks,' into which we fixed mop-sticks for barrels, kindly polished by 'Betty' with a *tinge* of blacklead, to make 'em look like *real* barrels.

The boys watched their fathers 'drill'; and 'as the old cock crows the young one learns,' so we children followed in the steps of our papas, and we were ready for inspection quite as soon as our elders, and could march in good order, to have *our* 'Field-day,' from Bloomsbury Church to the fields, where Russell and Tavistock Squares now stand.

Quoted from a pamphlet by Cruikshank in *The Life of George Cruikshank*, by Blanchard Jerrold, 1882.

born September 1768.

Lucile, my fourth sister, was two years older than myself. Like a neglected younger daughter, her dress consisted of the left-off clothes of her elder sisters. I leave the reader to imagine a very thin, little girl, too tall for her age, her arms swinging awkwardly at her sides, oppressed by timidity, as if afraid to speak, and unable to learn anything. Picture her dressed in a frock not made to fit her, her waist compressed by corsets, with whalebones running into her sides; – forced to hold her head erect by an iron collar covered with brown velvet; – her hair turned up and confined beneath a black toque: if the reader can imagine all this, he may be able to form some idea of the miserable little creature whom I beheld on my return to the paternal roof. Could I ever have conceived that she would one day be adorned with the talent and beauty which distinguished Lucile?

She was my playmate; or, rather, I was allowed to make her my plaything. I did not abuse my power. Instead of being her tyrant, I became her defender. Every morning, Lucile and I were taken to the Sisters Couppart, two old hunchbacked women dressed in black, who taught children to

read. Lucile was a bad scholar, and I, a worse one. The governesses scolded Lucile; I attacked the governesses. Serious complaints were, in consequence, carried to my mother. I began to be looked upon as a rebel, an idler, and a dunce. This ill opinion of me took a firm hold of the minds of my parents.

My father used to say, that not one of the Chevaliers de Chateaubriand had ever been remarkable for anything but sporting, drinking and brawling. My mother sighed and groaned when she happened to see my coat torn. My father's ill-temper disgusted me, and, when my mother summed up her remonstrances with the eulogy of my brother, calling him a Cato and a hero, I felt inclined to make myself as bad as it seemed I was expected to be.

Chateaubriand, *Memoirs*,
Translated London, 1848.

HARTLEY COLERIDGE
born September 1796.

The ground and *matériel* of this division of one's friends into *ac*, *con* and *in*quaintance, was given by Hartley Coleridge when he was scarcely five years old. On some one asking him if Anny Sealy (a little girl he went to school with) was an acquaintance of his, he replied, very fervently pressing his right hand on his heart, 'No, she is an *in*quaintance!' 'Well! 'tis a father's tale;' and the recollection soothes your old friend and *in*quaintance.

S. T. Coleridge,
Fraser's Magazine, 1835.

DERWENT COLERIDGE
born September 1800.

I cannot leave this period of my existence without some little allusion to my brother Derwent's sweet childhood. I have often heard from mama what a fine, fair, broad-chested little fellow he was at two years old, and how he got the name of Stumpy Canary when he wore a yellow frock, which made him look like one of these feathery bundles in colour and form. I fancy I see him now, as my mother's description brought him before me, racing from kitchen to parlour, and from parlour to kitchen, just putting in his head at the door, with roguish smile, to catch notice, then off again, shaking his little sides with laughter.

Memoir and Letters of Sarah Coleridge,
edited by her daughter, 1873.

LUCRETIA DAVIDSON
born September 1808.

When she was about nine, one of her schoolfellows gave her a young rat that had broken its leg in attempting to escape from a trap; she tore off a part of her pocket-handkerchief, bound up the maimed leg, carried the animal home, and nursed it tenderly. The rat, in spite of the care of its little leech, died, and was buried in the garden, and honoured with the meed of a 'melodious tear.' This lament has not been preserved; but

one she wrote soon after, on the death of a
maimed pet Robin, is given here as the earliest
record of her muse that has been preserved:

Underneath this turf doth lie
A little bird which ne'er could fly;
Twelve large angle worms did fill
This little bird, whom they did kill,
Puss! If you should chance to smell
My little bird from his dark cell,
Oh! do be merciful, my cat,
And not serve him as you did my rat!
                                        Sedgwick,
           Biography of Lucretia Davidson, 1848.

GAMES
for the
SEPTEMBER
BABY

FACE-TAPPING, the nurse tapping each feature as she sings these lines –
Here sits the lord mayor (forehead),
  Here sit his two men (eyes);
Here sits the cock (right cheek),
  Here sits the hen (left cheek).
Here sit the little chickens (tip of nose),
  Here they run in (mouth);
Chinchopper, chinchopper,
  Chinchopper, chin! (chucking the chin).
Popular Rhymes and Nursery Tales,
collected by Halliwell, 1849.

Bounce the baby on your knee to this rhythm:
To market, to market, to buy a fat pig;
Home again, home again, jiggety jig.
Ride to the market, to buy a fat hog;
Home again, home again, jiggety jog.
Nursery Rhymes, Tales and Jingles,
London: 1844.

THE FAMILY COACH. – There is one manager, who sits in the middle of the room; all the rest sit round in a circle. Each must take the name of some part of the coach, the horses, coachman, footman, lady or gentleman, or any part of the family in the coach. The manager must then tell an amusing story about the coach – where it was coming from, and where going; why going, who the passengers were, and various occurrences which happened to it on the road. Each time any part or person is mentioned, the player who represents it, must jump up and turn round once. If the '*whole coach*' is mentioned, every body must jump up and turn round. The great object of the manager should be to make the story so interesting that all are too much absorbed by it to recollect the portion of the coach they represent. Forfeits for mistakes.

Kingston, *Infant Amusements*, 1867.

A
SEPTEMBER
CHILD
IN
FICTION

WOLODA'S condescension gave us little satisfaction; on the contrary his lazy and tired expression destroyed the fun of the game. When we sat on the ground, and imagined that we were sitting in a boat and fishing or rowing with all our might, Woloda sat with folded hands and in a position which had nothing in common with that of a fisherman. I made a remark on this, but he answered that by our moving our hands more or less we should neither gain nor lose, and not advance a bit. I involuntarily agreed with him. When I pretended to go out hunting with a stick on my shoulder and went to the wood, Woloda lay on his back with his hands under his head, and said to me that it was all the same whether he went or not. Such behaviour and words, cooling our ardour for the game, were exceedingly disagreeable, the more so as it was impossible not to acknowledge to oneself that Woloda acted very wisely. I knew very well that it was not only impossible to kill birds with a stick, but to shoot with it at all. Still, just *this* was the play! If we once began to reason thus, then it was likewise impossible to drive on chairs; and I think Woloda himself must recollect how, on long winter evenings, we used to cover an arm-chair with a shawl and make a carriage of it, one of us being the coachman, another the footman, the girls sitting in it, three chairs being the 'Troika' of horses, and then how we pretended to set out. And what strange occurrences we used to meet with on our way! And how gaily and quickly those long winter evenings passed away! If we were always to judge from reality, those games would be nonsense; but if play were nonsense, what would be left?

Tolstoy, *Childhood and Youth*, translated from the Russian by Meysenbug, 1862.

LETTERS
from TWO
ROYAL SEPTEMBER
CHILDREN

MADAME,
I am struggling between two contending wishes; one is, my impatient desire to see your majesty, the other that of rendering the obedience I owe to the commands of the king my father, which prevent me from leaving my house till he has given me full permission to do so. But I hope that I shall be able shortly to gratify both these desires. In the meantime, I entreat your majesty to permit me to show, by this billet, the zeal with which I devote my respect to you as my queen, and my entire obedience to you as to my mother. I am too young and feeble to have power to do more than to felicitate you with all my heart in this

commencement of your marriage. I hope that your majesty will have as much goodwill for me, as I have zeal for your service.

Elizabeth I to Anne of Cleves.

Most illustrious and most excellent lady, my dearest spouse, I wish you very much health, with my hearty commendation.

I have read the most sweet letters of your highness lately given to me, from which I have easily perceived your most entire love to me. Truly those your letters, traced by your own hand, have so delighted me, and have rendered me so cheerful and jocund, that I fancied I beheld your highness and conversed with and embraced my dearest wife. I cannot tell you what an earnest desire I feel to see your highness, and how vexatious to me is this procrastination about your coming. I owe eternal thanks to your excellence that you so lovingly correspond to this my so ardent love. Let it continue, I entreat, as it has begun; and, like as I to cherish your sweet remembrance night and day, so do you preserve my name ever fresh in your breast. And let your coming to me be hastened, that instead of being absent we may be present with each other, and the love conceived between us and the wished-for joys may reap their proper fruit.

> From a letter of Arthur, Prince of Wales, aged thirteen, to his child fiancée, Catherine of Aragon.

RHYMES
for the
SEPTEMBER
BABY

WARM September brings the
    fruit;
Sportsmen then begin to
    shoot.
Sara Coleridge (1802–1852).

Beside yon straggling fence that skirts the way,
With blossomed furze unprofitably gay,
There, in his noisy mansion, skill'd to rule,
The village master taught his little school;
A man severe he was, and stern to view,
I knew him well, and every truant knew;
Well had the boding tremblers learned to trace
The day's disasters in his morning face;
Full well they laughed, with counterfeited
    glee,
At all his jokes, for many a joke had he;
Full well the busy whisper circling round,
Conveyed the dismal tidings when he
    frowned;

Yet he was kind, or if severe in aught,
The love he bore to learning was in fault;
The village all declared how much he knew;
'Twas certain he could write, and cypher too;
Lands he could measure, terms and tides
    presage,
And even the story ran that he could gauge.
In arguing too, the parson owned his skill,
For even tho' vanquished, he could argue still;
While words of learned length and thundering
    sound,
Amazed the gazing rustics ranged around;
And still they gazed, and still the wonder grew,
That one small head could carry all he knew.

from *The Deserted Village*,
by Oliver Goldsmith (1728–1774).

LULLABY

Sweet and low, sweet and low,
    Wind of the western sea,

Low, low, breathe and blow,
    Wind of the western sea!
Over the rolling waters go,
Come from the dying moon, and blow,
    Blow him again to me;
While my little one, while my pretty one,
        sleeps.

Sleep and rest, sleep and rest,
    Father will come to thee soon;
Rest, rest, on mother's breast,
    Father will come to thee soon;
Father will come to his babe in the nest,
Silver sails all out of the west
    Under the silver moon:
Sleep, my little one, sleep, my pretty one,
        sleep.

                    Tennyson (1809–1892).

A PRAYER

Teach me to do the thing that pleaseth
Thee, for Thou art my God.
                    The Girl's Little Book,
                by Charlotte M. Yonge, 1893.

GOODNIGHT
to the
SEPTEMBER
BABY

T HE day is over, and the stars are
coming out. If a star should, while
you are watching, fall, would you
wish, and if you wished what would you wish
for? Probably something for your September
baby, but what? Suppose when you were born
your mother had seen a star fall, and made a
wish for you, what would she have wished for,
and would you have been pleased? It is
amusing to think of how different your life
might have been due to a wish of your
mother's, if it could have come true, and it is
a subject for speculation if you would have
been as happy. Wishes have a queer way of
being granted in a different form to the way
pictured by the one who made the wish. Who

knows what exciting qualities are born in your baby, and how devastating if a well-meant wish upset the balance of its life? Wishing on a star for yourself is fun, but for another, no. In any case would you change anything about your baby if you could? Of course you wouldn't. So pleased and contented, goodnight – sleep well.

Noel Streatfeild